This Gift Belongs To...

From: _____

To: _____

Date: _____

"EVERY GOOD AND PERFECT GIFT COMES FROM ABOVE"

Show Me
To the Gates

By:

Evangelist Lynn Carol Ingram

SHOW ME TO THE GATES...

Edited by: Betty M. Thompson

Cover Design: SOS Graphic Designs

Published by: G Publishing LLC

ISBN: 978-0-9987663-2-4

Printed in the United States of America

"Lord God, Fill Me with your Holy Spirit"

~Dedication~

This book is dedicated to my *wonderful* husband, *Maurice O. Ingram Sr.*

The one I love and trust, Moe thank you for believing in me and trusting God's plan for our lives. To my brothers and sisters, my children and grandchildren, cousins, nieces, nephews, my aunt Joann Jones-Moses. Thank you all for the support and love you show daily. I love you with all my heart!

In memory of my parents ~ Voncile & Charlie Thompson

my Spiritual mother ~ Pearlie. Moncrief

"Lord God, Fill Me with your Holy Spirit"

SHOW ME TO THE GATES...

This book is design to be an easy read, an easy way of learning to pray and spend time with God. In life going into the new ~ is sometimes hard, what we have to do is "Just Do It" trust that God has your back and He will never leave you nor will He forsake you.

There will be some days where you feel you do not want to pray. That is when you pick up this book and just read a prayer that will place you in that spiritual place.

Ask God daily to fill you with his holy Spirit; The holy spirit will direct you in all things!

"PLEASE KNOW"

Ask, and it will be given to you;

Seek, and ye shall find;

Knock; and it will be opened unto you:

~Matt 7: 7

Let us be mindful to pray always. In good times and bad times.

Every prayer does not have to be 30 minutes long. We need to acknowledge God every day and as often as we can;

He's waiting to hear from us.

"Lord God, Fill Me with your Holy Spirit"

SHOW ME TO THE GATES...

"Confession"

Lord God I confess JESUS CHRIST as my personal savior. I believe he died on the cross for my sins and rose from the dead, and now seated in heaven at the right hand of God making intercession on my behalf.

The Bible tells me that, If I confess with my mouth and believe in my heart that You (God) raised Jesus from the dead, I shall be saved.

Thank you for saving me from damnation and destruction, In JESUS name,

Amen

"Lord God, Fill Me with your Holy Spirit"

SHOW ME TO THE GATES...

Call on the name that's above every name. "Jesus!"

"Lord God, Fill Me with your Holy Spirit"

Date: _____

when you begin writing

in your journal.

SHOW ME TO THE GATES...

Preparing for this journey requires discipline. Set aside a special time to spend getting to know your Father.

Try your hardest to stick to the plan, it will be the most rewarding and beneficial gift you've ever given to yourself!

"Lord God, Fill Me with your Holy Spirit"

SHOW ME TO THE GATES...

Before praying, make a list of people and things you want to pray for. This will help you keep focus.

_____

_____

_____

_____

_____

_____

"Lord God, Fill Me with your Holy Spirit"

SHOW ME TO THE GATES...

I've got a feeling everything is going to be alright!

"Lord God, Fill Me with your Holy Spirit"

SHOW ME TO THE GATES...

Let the words of my mouth and the meditation of my heart be acceptable in thy sight oh Lord my strength and my redeemer.

Oh, taste and see the Lord is good.

- I am seated in heavenly places with Jesus Christ.
- The Lord God is a sun and shield, He will give grace and glory, no good thing will He withhold from those who walk uprightly.
- I will always bless the Lord and His praise will continually be in my mouth.
- Be still and know that I and the Lord God: I shall be exalted among the heathen I shall be exalted among the earth.
- Cast your cares upon Him, for he cares for you.
- Seek the Lord while He may be found, call upon him while He is near!
- Call upon me in the days of trouble, I will answer.

I will sustain you I will rescue you.

- Everyone who calls on the name of the Lord will be saved.
- He will never let the righteous be shaken.
- Then you will call on me and come and pray to me and I will listen to you.

~ He is a rewarder to them that diligently seek Him ~

Hebrews 11: 6a.b

"Lord God, Fill Me with your Holy Spirit"

SHOW ME TO THE GATES...

Let's Pray!

"Lord God, Fill Me with your Holy Spirit"

SHOW ME TO THE GATES...

Lord God,

I come to you this day just to say, "thank you!"

I know I do not say it as often as I should, please forgive me.

I thank you for keeping me from this awful pandemic of COVID-19

in the year of 2020… WOW, what a year!!!

I thank you from keeping me from danger seen and unseen. I thank you for keeping me from losing my mind. I thank you for giving me opportunities to be a better me. I thank you for giving me a chance to make things right with you. I thank you for loving me, despite my faults. I thank you for life health and strength. I thank you for my family and my friends.

I am not asking for anything this day, but I am thanking you for everything you have done and are doing for me!

You, Lord have allowed me to come into your presence with thanksgiving in my heart to say thank you, thank you, thank you for all the many blessing you have poured out upon me and into me.

I love you; I honor you; I praise you; I thank you in Jesus precious name I pray….

AMEN

Casting your cares upon Him; for he careth for you.

1Peter 5: 7

"Lord God, Fill Me with your Holy Spirit"

SHOW ME TO THE GATES...

_____

_____

_____

_____

_____

_____

_____

_____

_____

"Lord God, Fill Me with your Holy Spirit"

SHOW ME TO THE GATES...

But, as it is written, Eye hath not seen, nor ear heard, nether have entered into the heart of man the things which God hath prepared for them that love him.

1Cor: 2: 9 Kjv

"Lord God, Fill Me with your Holy Spirit"

SHOW ME TO THE GATES...

_____

_____

_____

_____

_____

_____

_____

_____

_____

"Lord God, Fill Me with your Holy Spirit"

SHOW ME TO THE GATES...

Lord God,

I come asking that you would please prepare the hearts of your children for this new journey.

I know, you know the mindset of each one of us, help them to be open to each anointed word, prayer, and thought that comes to their mind. Lead them to a place of meditation and prayer time set apart for you Lord.

Surround them with angels of protection from heavens armies.

~ Pray this Prayer ~

I thank you for your divine covering as I sit in your presence; as your anointing pours out upon me, as I obtain knowledge, wisdom, strength, and change. Lord I thank you in advance for what I am about to experience. for I will never be the same!

Lord lead me, guide me, change me in Jesus precious name I pray,

AMEN

JESUS TAUGHT THIS PRAYER: OUR FATHER WHO ART IN HEAVEN...

MATT 6:9

"Lord God, Fill Me with your Holy Spirit"

SHOW ME TO THE GATES...

"Lord God, Fill Me with your Holy Spirit"

SHOW ME TO THE GATES...

Lord God,

I come to you confessing that Jesus is the Lord and savior of my life.

I ask that you forgive me of my sins… the known and unknown sins.

I surrender to your will for my life, save me from eternal damnation, wash me and cleanse me from all unrighteousness.

I confess that Jesus died for my sin and were raised from the dead, so that I may be saved!

With this confession, I believe that I am saved, and I am now a joint-heir with Jesus Christ. Thank you, Lord God,

In Jesus Christ name I pray this prayer,

AMEN

After this manner there pray ye: Our Father which art in heaven, Hallowed be thy name….

Matt 6:9

"Lord God, Fill Me with your Holy Spirit"

SHOW ME TO THE GATES...

_____

_____

_____

_____

_____

_____

_____

_____

_____

"Lord God, Fill Me with your Holy Spirit"

SHOW ME TO THE GATES...

COME CLOSE TO GOD AND GOD WILL COME CLOSE TO YOU...

James 4: 8a NLT

_____

_____

_____

_____

_____

_____

_____

_____

"Lord God, Fill Me with your Holy Spirit"

SHOW ME TO THE GATES...

_____

_____

_____

_____

_____

_____

_____

_____

_____

_____

"Lord God, Fill Me with your Holy Spirit"

SHOW ME TO THE GATES...

Write the vision and make it plan on tablets

Habakkuk 2:2

_____

_____

_____

_____

_____

_____

_____

_____

"Lord God, Fill Me with your Holy Spirit"

SHOW ME TO THE GATES...

_____
_____
_____
_____
_____
_____
_____
_____
_____
_____

"Lord God, Fill Me with your Holy Spirit"

SHOW ME TO THE GATES...

POUR OUT YOU HEART TO GOD

_____

_____

_____

_____

_____

_____

_____

_____

"Lord God, Fill Me with your Holy Spirit"

SHOW ME TO THE GATES...

_____

_____

_____

_____

_____

_____

_____

_____

_____

_____

"Lord God, Fill Me with your Holy Spirit"

SHOW ME TO THE GATES...

Lord God,

Here I am writing another prayer... Thank you for bringing me this far.

So far, I have written a few prayers, I'm smiling right now(Smile) because how far I've come.

Thank you so much for working on me! There is a lot on my mind, and I don't know where to start, my prayers maybe everywhere. However, I know you understand what I am saying, and I know You knows my heart.

Thank you so much for this time of working in me as well as working on me.

I will continue to set aside time to pray and read my bible. It's hard sometimes with everything that's going the way it has been in my life but, I'm doing it.

Until my next prayer God thank you for listing and I love you!

In Jesus name I pray,

Amen

"Lord God, Fill Me with your Holy Spirit"

SHOW ME TO THE GATES...

_____

_____

_____

_____

_____

_____

_____

_____

_____

"Lord God, Fill Me with your Holy Spirit"

SHOW ME TO THE GATES...

_____

_____

_____

_____

_____

_____

_____

_____

_____

"Lord God, Fill Me with your Holy Spirit"

SHOW ME TO THE GATES...

There is Nothing Too Hard for God

You can ask for anything in my name, and I will do it, so that the Son can bring glory to the Father.

John 14: 13 ~ NLT

"Lord God, Fill Me with your Holy Spirit"

SHOW ME TO THE GATES...

Lord God,
There are some things I want to accomplish this year, God I need you to guide me through, I know I can't do this on my own. With you on my side I know I cannot fail. I am pressing forward leaving some people behind. I know for me to grow I can't keep what's not good for me in my life. I am so proud of whom I am becoming! Now things are easy for me to let go, such as... the wrong things and people.
Continue to bless and keep me in your will. in Jesus name I pray,

Amen

"Lord God, Fill Me with your Holy Spirit"

SHOW ME TO THE GATES...

Write what you want God to change or do in your life...

_____

_____

_____

_____

_____

_____

_____

_____

"Lord God, Fill Me with your Holy Spirit"

SHOW ME TO THE GATES...

Not by might nor by power, but by my Spirit says the Lord of host.

"Lord God, Fill Me with your Holy Spirit"

SHOW ME TO THE GATES...

I will bless the Lord at all times, and His praise shall continually be in my mouth;

"Lord God, Fill Me with your Holy Spirit"

SHOW ME TO THE GATES...

Lord God,

I know I can tell you anything because you are listing. I can tell you all my deep dark secrets, the parts I don't want anyone to know!

"Lord I'm messed up!" I really need you right now to touch me, show me how to live this thing called life! I am not happy with the way I am, teach me, show me how to love unconditionally, show me what I'm doing wrong?

I need you Jesus; I need your help JESUS!

I surrender to you, I'm tired of living this way. I want to be right; I want to drop all these bad habits; I want to have a clean heart a pure heart. Have mercy on me Jesus. I've tried my way it doesn't seem to work! deliver me from the things of this world that's not good for me. Remove the people that is not supposed to be in my life. Remove these evil thoughts from my head. Help me God!

I'm going to keep calling on your name until my change comes!

Jesus, Jesus, Jesus the more I call on you the better I feel! I need deliverance Jesus., I need your help, I need you.

Amen

"Lord God, Fill Me with your Holy Spirit"

SHOW ME TO THE GATES...

Change Me God

_____

_____

_____

_____

_____

_____

_____

_____

_____

_____

"Lord God, Fill Me with your Holy Spirit"

SHOW ME TO THE GATES...

Have mercy upon me, O God. According to thy lovingkindness: according unto the multitude of thy tender mercies blot out my transgressions.

Wash me thoroughly from mine iniquity, and cleanse me from my sin.

For I acknowledge my transgressions: and my sin is ever before me. Against thee, thee only, have I sinned and done this evil in thy sight: that thou might be justified when thou speak, and be clear when thou judges.

Behold, I was shapen in iniquity; and in sin did my mother conceive me.

Behold, thou desires truth in the inward part: and in the hidden part thou shall make me to know wisdom.

Purge me with hyssop, and I shall be clean: wash me and I shall be whiter than snow.

Make me to hear joy and gladness; that the bones which thou have broken may rejoice.

Hide thy face from my sins and blot out all mine iniquities.

Create in me a clean heart, O God; and renew a right Spirit within me.

Cast me not away from thy presence; and take not thy holy spirit from me. Restore the joy of your salvation and uphold me with thy free spirit.

Psalms 51: 1-12

"Lord God, Fill Me with your Holy Spirit"

SHOW ME TO THE GATES...

_____

_____

_____

_____

_____

_____

_____

_____

_____

"Lord God, Fill Me with your Holy Spirit"

Lord forgive us of our sin knowing, and unknowing. Fix me Jesus, Fix me!

"Lord God, Fill Me with your Holy Spirit"

SHOW ME TO THE GATES...

Just Pray...

"Lord God, Fill Me with your Holy Spirit"

Show Me

To

The Gates

"Lord God, Fill Me with your Holy Spirit"

SHOW ME TO THE GATES...

Peace Be Still!

"Lord God, Fill Me with your Holy Spirit"

SHOW ME TO THE GATES...

Hear My Prayer Oh God!

_____

_____

_____

_____

_____

_____

_____

_____

"Lord God, Fill Me with your Holy Spirit"

SHOW ME TO THE GATES...

I'm no longer doing it my way, God Take control

_____

_____

_____

_____

_____

_____

_____

_____

"Lord God, Fill Me with your Holy Spirit"

SHOW ME TO THE GATES...

There are some things that I can only tell you God...

_____

_____

_____

_____

_____

_____

_____

_____

"Lord God, Fill Me with your Holy Spirit"

And He said to me, My grace is sufficient for thee, for my strength is made perfect in weakness. Most gladly therefore will I rather glory in my infirmities, that the power of Christ may rest upon me.

SHOW ME TO THE GATES...

search me Oh God, and know my heart, try me, and know my thoughts: ~ *Psalm 139 23-24*

_____

_____

_____

_____

_____

_____

_____

_____

"Lord God, Fill Me with your Holy Spirit"

SHOW ME TO THE GATES...

Lord God,

I woke up this morning with you on my mind, thanking you for another day. Thanking you for my family, thanking you for blessing us and keeping us, thanking you for healing us, thanking you for binding us together in love.

Lord, I absolutely love you, and for all the ways you have made, the doors you've opened and closed ~ the favor on my life, you did it all for me... I'm so grateful for you sparring not only my life but my family's to!

God, I am asking that you continue to do what you do in my life and the lives of my love ones!

IN JESUS NAME I PRAY, AMEN

"Lord God, Fill Me with your Holy Spirit"

SHOW ME TO THE GATES...

_____

_____

_____

_____

_____

_____

_____

_____

_____

"Lord God, Fill Me with your Holy Spirit"

SHOW ME TO THE GATES...

Order My Steps...

_____

_____

_____

_____

_____

_____

_____

_____

Parrice Ingram- Williams

"Lord God, Fill Me with your Holy Spirit"

SHOW ME TO THE GATES...

"Spirit of the living God fall fresh on me"

_____

_____

_____

_____

_____

_____

_____

_____

~Tameika S, Thompson

"Lord God, Fill Me with your Holy Spirit"

SHOW ME TO THE GATES...

"Lord God, Fill Me with your Holy Spirit"

SHOW ME TO THE GATES...

He prepares a table in the presence of mine enemy,

_____

_____

_____

_____

_____

_____

_____

_____

Steven Von-Charles

"Lord God, Fill Me with your Holy Spirit"

SHOW ME TO THE GATES...

_____

_____

_____

_____

_____

_____

_____

_____

_____

"Lord God, Fill Me with your Holy Spirit"

SHOW ME TO THE GATES...

Prayer is always needed in every situation, call upon the name of Jesus.

_____

_____

_____

_____

_____

_____

_____

_____

~Shameika Thompson

"Lord God, Fill Me with your Holy Spirit"

SHOW ME TO THE GATES...

"*Lord God, Fill Me with your Holy Spirit*"

SHOW ME TO THE GATES...

Gear up for the battle; Put on the whole armor of God.

Eph 6: 11

_____

_____

_____

_____

_____

_____

_____

_____

~Bro. Maurice O. Ingram Sr.

"Lord God, Fill Me with your Holy Spirit"

2020

The nation is called to pray against the Coronavirus – COVID 19

As a praying Christian woman, I say satin the BLOOD OF JESUS IS AGAINST YOU!

Continue to pray and cover our country the whole world and it's decision making leaders.

"Lord God, Fill Me with your Holy Spirit"

SHOW ME TO THE GATES...

"Lord God, Fill Me with your Holy Spirit"

SHOW ME TO THE GATES...

You are fearfully and wonderfully made...
                              Psalm 139: 14

Never speak negative over your life or anyone connected to you, and never allow anyone to speak negativity over your life.

"Lord God, Fill Me with your Holy Spirit"

SHOW ME TO THE GATES...

The name of the Lord is a strong tower; the righteous run in and they are safe.

_____

_____

_____

_____

_____

_____

_____

_____

~ Betty Thompson

"Lord God, Fill Me with your Holy Spirit"

SHOW ME TO THE GATES...

I will grow from the things I have encountered in this life.

"Lord God, Fill Me with your Holy Spirit"

SHOW ME TO THE GATES...

The joy of the Lord is my strength,

_____

_____

_____

_____

_____

_____

_____

_____

~Min. Carla Carrington

"Lord God, Fill Me with your Holy Spirit"

Pray on…

in the name that's above

every name, "Jesus"

Power falls when you

call Him!

"Lord God, Fill Me with your Holy Spirit"

SHOW ME TO THE GATES...

Bless Me Lord, Like Only You Can!"

~Telly Thompson

"Lord God, Fill Me with your Holy Spirit"

SHOW ME TO THE GATES...

Pray Until Something Happens!

_____

_____

_____

_____

_____

_____

_____

_____

~Lela A. Poole

"Lord God, Fill Me with your Holy Spirit"

SHOW ME TO THE GATES...

It's not over until God says it Over

_____

_____

_____

_____

_____

_____

_____

_____

~Lexus Haroya'

"Lord God, Fill Me with your Holy Spirit"

SHOW ME TO THE GATES...

You got this now… Pray!!!

_____

_____

_____

_____

_____

_____

_____

_____

Illya T.

"Lord God, Fill Me with your Holy Spirit"

SHOW ME TO THE GATES...

Pray until you get your breakthrough!

"Lord God, Fill Me with your Holy Spirit"

SHOW ME TO THE GATES...

Being confident of this very thing, that He who has begun a good work in you will complete it until the day of Jesus Christ;

Philippians 1: 6

~Tameika Thompson

"Lord God, Fill Me with your Holy Spirit"

SHOW ME TO THE GATES...

Now that I made it this far nothing can stop me now!

Because the Bible says: What, shall we say in response to these things? If God be for us, who can be against us?

_____

_____

_____

_____

_____

_____

_____

_____

Stephanie La'tia

"Lord God, Fill Me with your Holy Spirit"

SHOW ME TO THE GATES...

Lord God,

I come praying for marriages, protect them from divorce, separation, and miscommunication! I plead the blood of Jesus Christ over every couple you have drown together.

I declare we will love one another, respect, listen to, protect, become a safe place for our spouse, in Jesus precious name... your will shall be done in our lives! And I is so! Amen

Mark 10: 9

~Santarilla Thompson

"Lord God, Fill Me with your Holy Spirit"

SHOW ME TO THE GATES...

_____

_____

_____

_____

_____

_____

_____

_____

_____

"Lord God, Fill Me with your Holy Spirit"

SHOW ME TO THE GATES...

Lord God,

I am Praying for healing,

I'm Praying for the grieving,

I'm Praying for our children,

I'm Praying you supply all our need...

I'm Praying over our spouse,

I'm Praying for Pastors,

I'm Praying for the Leaders of this world,

I'm Praying for my family ~ friends,

I'm Praying over our homes,

Lord I am praying...

I'm Praying for the elderly,

I'm praying, I'm praying...

"Lord listen to your children praying,

Send us love, send us power and grace!

James K. Thompson

"Lord God, Fill Me with your Holy Spirit"

I love the Lord, He Heard my cry and pitted my every groan, Long as I live, and trouble rise; I'll hasten to His throne!

"Lord God, Fill Me with your Holy Spirit"

SHOW ME TO THE GATES...

The

Gates

Are

Open....

"Lord God, Fill Me with your Holy Spirit"

SHOW ME TO THE GATES...

"Lord God, Fill Me with your Holy Spirit"

SHOW ME TO THE GATES...

Give yourself some praise, for how far you have come in life!

_____

_____

_____

_____

_____

_____

_____

_____

~Jammie L. Thompson

"Lord God, Fill Me with your Holy Spirit"

SHOW ME TO THE GATES...

"Lord God, Fill Me with your Holy Spirit"

SHOW ME TO THE GATES...

Congratulations... You done it; you have finished the journey you have started!

Now stay the course, read pray, and study your Bible,

Meditate on God daily You will overcome all ossicles. God loves you. May I also remind you?

The decisions you make today will affect your tomorrow!

Therefore, my beloved brethren, Be Steadfast, unmovable, always abounding in the work of the Lord, forasmuch as ye know that your labor is not in vain in the Lord.

1Cor. 15:58

"Lord God, Fill Me with your Holy Spirit"

SHOW ME TO THE GATES...

"Lord God, Fill Me with your Holy Spirit"

Show Me
To The
Gates!

"Lord God, Fill Me with your Holy Spirit"

SHOW ME TO THE GATES...

Now unto Him that is able to do exceeding abundantly above all that we ask or think, according to the power that worketh in us. Unto Him be glory in the church by Christ Jesus throughout all ages, world without all end.

Amen

Eph 3:20

"Lord God, Fill Me with your Holy Spirit"

SHOW ME TO THE GATES...

"*Lord God, Fill Me with your Holy Spirit*"

www.ingramcontent.com/pod-product-compliance
Lightning Source LLC
Chambersburg PA
CBHW061415090426
42742CB00026B/3478